Contents

G000135520

1 On the edge of the known world?

In 1972, Ireland joined the European Community. Twenty years later the Channel Tunnel linked Britain to the mainland of Europe. Now Ireland is the only country in the community which does not have a land-link with the others. Many people worry that this will leave her out of touch. But has Ireland always been like that? This book tells the story of Ireland from around AD 600 to 1169 (the year the Normans first came). Was Ireland in those days looked on as part of Europe? Did the Irish people see themselves as Europeans or as 'dwellers at the edge of the earth'?

A An astronaut's view of Ireland and Europe

1 *Find the Atlantic Ocean, Iceland, Greenland, the coast of North America.*

2 *Before Europeans sailed over the Atlantic to discover these places, which country did they think was on the edge of the world?*

In the seventh century, nearly fourteen hundred years ago, the best-known Irishman in Europe was St Columbanus. In AD 613 he was in Italy and wrote to the Pope, telling him about Ireland. He said that Christianity was strong among 'all us Irish, who are dwellers at the edge of the earth'. Over a hundred years later a famous English monk called Bede described the Irish as 'a little community, isolated at the furthest ends of the world'.

Columbanus and Bede were writing about what people in Europe believed was a 'fact'. Ireland stuck out in the sea on the far edge of the world. You could go no further west. Europeans expected the Irish to be different from other people, and liked to think of them as 'barbarians' or wild and uncivilised. It came as a surprise when they found that this was not always true.

Perhaps the greatest scholar in Europe in the ninth century was an Irishman, John Scotus Eriugena. There is a drawing of him on the Irish five-pound note. Because John had a great knowledge of Greek, the Holy Roman Emperor asked him to translate a very important book from Greek into Latin. When he was finished, the Pope's librarian was asked to say if he had done a good job.

B The librarian's letter to the Emperor, AD 860

3 *In what ways had John Scotus done a good job?*

4 *Why should the librarian be so surprised at his work?*

"It is a wonderful thing how that barbarian, living at the ends of the earth – who would be expected to be far removed even from knowledge of that language [Greek], let alone from its familiar use – has been able to understand such ideas and translate them into another tongue [that is, Latin]."

The librarian was surprised that Irish people could still be in close contact with Europe even though Ireland was far away. The Holy Roman Emperors knew better. The greatest of them was Charlemagne, who died in 814. We still have a book written at that time which tells us that the Irish kings wrote to Charlemagne with messages of their respect for him.

One of the ways in which Irish people came into contact with Europe was through the Church. Christianity had grown strong in Ireland and many Irish people took up the religious life and went off to live in monasteries. Irish monks set out to be missionaries in Britain and Europe, building new monasteries and churches wherever they went.

In recent times, many Irish people have been forced to emigrate to find work, but the early Christian monks chose to go overseas. Nearly twelve hundred years ago a monk in a monastery at Lake Constance (on the modern Swiss-German border), wrote about 'the Irish people, with whom the custom of travelling into foreign lands has become almost second nature'!

As Irish missionaries and scholars settled all over Europe, the fame of their monasteries and teachers in Ireland spread. So there was travel in the other direction, and people from other countries, especially Britain, came to live here in large numbers. In this way, in spite of its position, Ireland came to be part of Europe and made an important contribution to it.

1 *Why did people think that Ireland was a strange place? Why did they think that somebody like John Scotus Eriugena was a 'barbarian'?*

2 *For discussion: Ireland is still 'a little community, isolated at the furthest ends of the world'.*

What did Ireland look like in AD 600?

Even in our lifetime Ireland has changed a great deal. Imagine how much more it has changed in the past fourteen hundred years. So, going back to the year 600 what was Ireland like then? How different was it from the Ireland of today?

Forests

Ireland's mountains, plains, rivers and lakes have changed little since AD 600, but the dense forests which covered the country until a few hundred years ago have disappeared. Today Ireland is one of the most treeless regions in Europe.

A A round fort at Derryboy near Downpatrick, County Down

1 *What is growing in the fields round the fort?*
2 *'Derry' comes from the Irish word* doire, *which is an oak wood in English. What was growing here in Derryboy long ago?*

B Account from the *Annals*

3 *How has Derry and the land around changed since 1146?*

"1146 AD . . . There was a great wind-storm on the third of December, which caused great damage to woods all over Ireland. It knocked down sixty trees in Doire Choluim Cille."

(From the *Annals of the Four Masters*)

Over one thousand places in Ireland have 'doire' or 'derry' as part of their name. The most famous is Derry city, which was originally *Doire Choluim Cille* (St Colum Cille's oakwood). Fourteen hundred years ago such places were covered with oak forests. Over the years, people have cut the trees down just as the rainforests in South America are being destroyed today. They farmed in the spaces they cleared, and used the wood for burning and building.

Travelling by road

Armies needed roads to march across the country but these were not like today's roads. A main road was called a *slige* which means 'a cutting down', and so they were paths cut through the forests. We still have a 'glossary' or dictionary written about AD 900 by a man called Cormac, who says that a *slige* was wide enough for two chariots to pass. Nowadays the Irish word for a road is a *bóthar*, but Cormac tells us that this was a narrow path, only wide enough for two cows to pass when one was sideways!

Travelling by boat

Many people preferred to travel by boat on the rivers and lakes and to use the sea to get from one part of Ireland to another. The boats were usually rowing boats or currachs like those still found in the west of Ireland. The Irish also sailed bigger boats with a mast and sail. St Brendan the Navigator is said to have sailed to America nearly a thousand years before Christopher Columbus. A book describing his voyages became one of the most popular in Europe.

C Early Irish boats

4 *What materials were used for making boats? Where were they obtained? Why were hides 'tanned'? What was the fat for?*

5 *What power was used for these boats?*

C1 "Saint Brendan and those with him got iron tools and built a light boat ribbed with wood and with a wooden frame . . . They covered it with ox-hides tanned with the bark of oak and smeared all the joints of the hides on the outside with fat . . . They also placed a mast in the middle of the boat and a sail and the other requirements for steering a boat."

(From *The Voyage of St Brendan*, written about AD 800)

C2 "AD 891 Three Irishmen came to King Alfred, in a boat without any oars, from Ireland, which they had left because they wished, for the love of God, to be on pilgrimage, and did not care where. The boat in which they had set out was made of two and a half hides, and they had taken with them supplies for a week. And after a week they came to land in Cornwall . . . "

(From the *Anglo-Saxon Chronicle*)

Towns

Kings and lords gave the monasteries farmland where many people worked to supply the monks and nuns with food, leather and wool. Around the monasteries the monks and the families that lived nearby bought and sold food and other goods in markets. These settlements could not be called towns but they were the homes of thousands of Irish people. Many more people lived scattered about the country-side.

1 *Write a travel-guide to help visitors coming to Ireland for the first time in AD 600.*

2 *Make lists of the things that have got better and worse since the year 600. Would you prefer to live now or then?*

3 Early Irish society: Civilised or savage?

We have seen that many people long ago thought that Ireland was a strange, 'barbaric' place. This was partly because it was so far away but also because the way of life in Ireland was very different from the way people lived in other countries. In what way was it different? How was Irish society organised?

The legal system

Every country has a system of laws for organising the way people live. The legal system used in Ireland today was first brought here from England by the Normans about 800 years ago. Those laws gradually took the place of the old Irish system, called the Brehon laws from the Irish word *breitheamh*, which means a judge. In the seventh and eighth centuries the Brehon laws were set down in law-books by the highly trained lawyers of the time.

A A page from a Brehon law-book

This page was copied in the fourteenth century from a much older book. The smaller writing is where the later lawyer tries to explain what the old law means.

1 *What is important about old books like this? What can we learn from them that an archaeologist cannot find from digging up remains?*

2 *List five laws we have in Ireland today. What will a historian in the year 3000 learn from them about Ireland in the 1990s?*

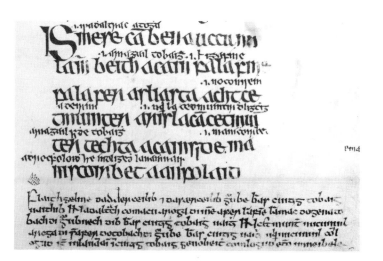

The Brehon law-books spelled out the rights and duties of everyone; from powerful kings to humble servants, from poets and doctors to blacksmiths and comb-makers, from women and children to people who were mentally ill and senile old folk.

B A penalty under the Brehon law

3 *Explain why this was an important law for its time.*

"Whoever kills a dog used for guarding the flocks must pay five cows for the dog, and supply a new dog of the same breed in its place. Also, until the end of the year, he must restore any of the flock that get eaten by wild animals."

(From the *Senchas Már*, eighth century)

Today, laws set out how individuals should behave. Under the Brehon laws, it was not the individual who mattered but the family or *fine*. If a person did something wrong, the whole *fine* was held responsible. If a man was murdered, it was the job of the *fine* to seek revenge or claim an *éraic* (compensation) for the death from the *fine* of the killer. The family group that mattered most was the *derbfine*. Your *derbfine* was made up of those descended from your great-grandfather in the male line. The female line was not recognised because when a woman married her children were part of her husband's *fine*. If a man died without an heir, his property was divided evenly between the *derbfine*.

4 *Draw up a family tree of your own* derbfine.

Classes of society

In Brehon law, there were three separate classes: kings, lords and commoners. A person's exact position in this arrangement was vital. Ireland was split into many small kingdoms. If a king was just and good, people believed that his kingdom would be peaceful and prosperous. If he was not, they said, even nature would turn against the kingdom. The weather would turn bad, disease would spread, animals would sicken and crops would fail.

The law said that a king should never do manual work or his 'honour-price' would fall. The honour-price measured a person's position on the social ladder. If someone seriously injured the king, or stole something from him, or refused him hospitality, his *fine* had to pay the victim his honour-price. A king of a whole province had an honour-price of 42 milking-cows, whereas a poor man's honour-price might be as little as a one-year-old heifer.

After the king came the wealthy lords. A lord had a number of 'clients'. The lord protected the client from enemies and gave him the use of land, cows or farm equipment. The client would serve in his lord's army, give him a share of the food he grew, help on his land at harvesting, and provide a feast when the lord visited.

There were many kinds of commoners, some wealthy and others who were little more than labourers. Some descended from lords whose families had lost their lands by war or bad luck with farming. Outside the three ranks of society there were unfree people who had no land and few belongings. They included serfs who had hardly any rights and simply worked on their lords' estates. Then there were slaves who could be bought and sold by their masters.

1 *Today all people are equal in the eyes of the law. How was the Brehon law different?*

2 *Describe the difference in the way that a Brehon judge and a modern judge decide on punishments for guilty people. Which would be more likely to cut down crime? Which method is fairer?*

4 What was the language of Ireland?

In Ireland today, most people speak English. Ireland is famous for its writers in English, such as James Joyce and Oscar Wilde and for poets like W. B. Yeats and Seamus Heaney. But many people prefer to use the Irish language, or Gaelic as it is often called. What language did the people use in Ireland fourteen hundred years ago? How important were its writers and what they wrote?

The beginnings of writing in Irish

The earliest traces of writing in Irish are more than fifteen hundred years old. It is a form of writing called Ogam, found on stones and pillars. People cut sets of notches, each standing for a letter of the alphabet, into the edge of the stone. The Christian monks who came to Ireland, however, used Latin. As more and more people became Christian the use of Latin spread. People began to use the Roman letters which are still used for writing in Irish and English today, so that gradually people stopped writing Ogam.

The famous Irish saint, Colum Cille, died in the year 597. Shortly afterwards a poet named Dallán Forgaill wrote a poem in his memory called *Amra Coluim Cille*. It may be the oldest poem in Europe in a language used for everyday speech. The poems which are older were written in Greek or Latin. These languages were mostly used in literature or for documents to do with government. The people who could read and write them often spoke a different language in their everyday life.

A **A copy of *Amra Coluim Cille* written down about AD 1100**

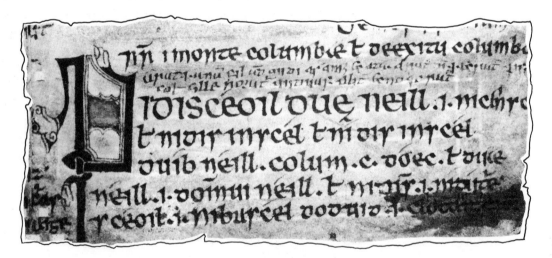

1 *See if you can make out any of the writing.*
2 *What language is used in the poem?*
3 *The capital letter is an 'N'. Try drawing it.*
4 *Part of Colum Cille's name is given three lines from the bottom. See if you can find it.*

(First line: Ni discéoil due Neil [Not good news for the Uí Néill])

The place of poets in Irish society

In the Ireland of fourteen hundred years ago there was a special class of people called the *áes dána*. The *áes dána* was made up of the Brehon lawyers, as well as the historians and the genealogists who kept a record of the family trees of kings and nobles. Poets were also part of the *áes dána*. They were held in great respect, but they were feared when they threatened to write a poem which mocked or put a curse on someone. Such a mocking poem was called a satire.

The sagas

It was at this time that the great Irish sagas were written down. Many are still well known, such as he stories of Cú Chulainn and the *Táin Bó Cúailgne* (The Cattle-raid of Cooley), of Oisín in *Tír na nÓg*, of Fionn and the Fianna, and of Cormac Mac Airt, the king of Tara. One of the loveliest in all Irish literature is the tale of Deirdre and the sons of Uisnech.

It tells how Deirdre, the most beautiful young woman in Ireland, was betrothed to Conor, the old king of Ulster. One day she was watching a dead calf being skinned when a raven began to drink the blood dripping on to the snow. 'I shall love the man who has those three colours,' said Deirdre, 'hair like a raven, cheeks like blood, and a body like snow.'

That man was Naoise, son of Uisnech, with whom she eloped to Scotland. King Conor invited them back pretending to forgive them, but when they came to Conor's palace at Emain Macha (Navan fort, near Armagh), he tricked them and Naoise and his brothers were slain. Deirdre stayed with the wicked King Conor for a year, but for all that time 'she neither smiled, nor ate nor slept her fill, nor raised her head from her knee'. In the end, in despair, she threw herself from her chariot, dashed her head on a rock, and followed Naoise to the grave.

Irish or English?

When the first Normans arrived in Ireland from Britain in 1169 some Norman lords spoke French and the soldiers, farmers and traders who came with them spoke English. The English language has been spoken in Ireland ever since but most Irish people continued to speak their own language until the last two hundred years or so.

As the two languages have lived side by side, there have been many arguments about whether English should replace Irish or whether Irish people should keep their own language.

---

1 *Make a list of five things you have learned about the Irish language in this Unit. Explain which one you think is most important.*

2 *What are the arguments for and against keeping the Irish language alive?*

5 The homes of the people: What traces survive?

Most of what we have learned so far about Ireland a thousand or more years ago we know from old hand-written books, called manuscripts. However, manuscripts are very scarce and they do not tell us all we would like to know. We can find out much more about some things by looking at the countryside around us. What traces of early Ireland can still be seen? Are any of the homes of the people who lived then still standing today?

A A ring-fort and a crannog, Lisleitrim, County Armagh

1 *Which is the ring-fort? How did it get its name?*

2 *What difficulties would there be for anyone fighting their way into the centre?*

3 *The crannog was in a good position for defence. Why?*

4 *Would these be the homes of wealthy or poor people?*

Ring-forts

Ordinary people's houses of a thousand or more years ago have almost completely disappeared but we can find the remains of where rich and powerful people lived. These were the ring-forts and crannogs. Ring-forts like the one in the picture often had as many as three ditches and banks. The ditches were up to two metres deep, sometimes filled with water. The banks between them were made up of earth taken from the ditches and may have had a fence or palisade on top.

A ring-fort made of earth is called a *rath* and the area inside it where the owner and his followers lived is the *lios*. In parts of the country where the land is stony the ring-fort was made with stone walls and is called a *caiseal* or *cathair*. Sometimes a very large ring-fort is called a *dún*. The fort in the picture is a *rath* with a *lios* in the centre which is where the first part of the name Lisleitrim comes from. Wherever you find places with the words *lis(s), ra(t)h, cashel, caher,* and *dun/doon* in their names you will usually find there was a ring-fort nearby.

Until recently there may have been the remains of as many as 60,000 ring-forts scattered throughout Ireland. But more and more are being destroyed as farmers improve their lands or as houses and roads are built. It has been calculated that 44 per cent of the ring-forts in County Kerry have disappeared in this way.

Ring-forts were really the farms of early medieval Ireland. The farm-houses and farm-buildings would have been at the centre and they would have been no cleaner than a modern farmyard. An old Irish story called 'The Feast of Bricriu' describes how Bricriu and his wife fell among the dogs lying on the dung-hill in the middle of the *lios*. Outside the fort would be the milking-yard, the mill for the corn (if the owners were rich enough to afford one), and the huts of servants. Stretching beyond them would be the fields where crops were grown and pastures for grazing animals.

Ring-forts were usually made in places where the land was worth farming and they were often on the top of a small hill with a good view of the countryside. This may have been to provide a look-out for approaching enemies but the site may also have been chosen to show off the owners' wealth. At that time people took care to display the position they had in society.

Crannogs

Crannogs or lake-dwellings are less common than ring-forts. There may be about 1,200 of them in the country. Some of them were natural islands, but many were man-made. This meant they were harder and more expensive to build than a ring-fort but they provided better defence, because to enter them you would have to use a boat or perhaps a wooden bridge or causeway (a raised path). As they were costly to make, we can be fairly sure that they were the well-defended homes of powerful people. We know for certain that some were the palaces of kings.

B **A modern experiment to work out how crannogs were built**

5 *What materials have been used?*

6 *What would have been the main difficulties in building a crannog?*

7 *Describe its defences.*

---

1 *Compare the crannog and the* rath *in the first picture. Which would be easier to defend if you lived inside it? Which would give the best chance for the poorer people nearby to take shelter if their land was attacked?*

2 *Where is the nearest ring-fort or crannog to you? What can you learn from it about life in early Ireland?*

3 *Many ring-forts are under threat from modern development. Should anything be done to protect those that have not yet been destroyed?*

6 What was life on the land like?

The picture we have of life in Ireland long ago comes partly from ancient manuscripts and partly from looking at remains in the landscape. When archaeologists dig up old sites they can find out a great deal more. If we put all the information together, what can we learn about life on the land, early farming and food?

Pastoral farming

A Archaeological evidence

1 *Turn this into a bar-chart showing cattle, pigs, sheep, working animals and hunted animals.*

2 *What does this tell you about the lives of people at Lagore?*

3 *Which animals would provide food only and which gave food and useful materials?*

Animal skulls found at a crannog at Lagore in County Meath, home of local kings from the seventh to the tenth century.

Cattle skulls	608	Red-deer skulls	4
Pig skulls	173	Fox skulls	2
Sheep skulls	153	Hare skulls	1
Horse skulls	9	Otter skulls	1
Dog skulls	7	Heron skulls	1
		Total	959

At the time when kings lived in Lagore, there was no money, so often people worked out the cost of goods or the amount of a fine in cows. In the summer they normally lived on milk and dairy products such as butter, cheese, curds and whey. Salt was used to preserve these foods and even today archaeologists dig up salty Irish butter that was buried in bogs a thousand or more years ago to keep it fresh and safe!

In the autumn a few cattle were killed and the beef was salted to eat in winter, but most of the meat came from pigs, who ate the mast (acorns and other nuts) from the trees in the woods. Sheep were kept mostly for wool, not for mutton. Horses were small, rather like the Connemara ponies of today. People kept dogs as working animals and as pets. At Lagore archaeologists found the bones of Irish wolf-hounds, sheep-dogs, large terriers, spaniels, and little lap-dogs.

Arable farming

'Arable' comes from the Latin word for ploughing (*arare*, to plough) and we use it to describe crop-farming. Some arable farming was done in all parts of Ireland, but it was usually not as important as pastoral farming. The main crops were oats (for bread, porridge and gruel), barley (for beer and also bread) and wheat (for wheaten bread, which was a luxury). Families had vegetable patches and apple orchards but they also collected wild fruit and nuts and kept bees.

Famine and disease

Since Irish people had both crops and animals they were safe from hunger if only one was scarce. If animals were stolen or hit by disease in the same year that crops were destroyed by bad weather or an enemy army then famine followed. Food shortages made people less able to stand up to diseases which spread easily because of bad hygiene. Every few years many people would die from dysentery, influenza, small-pox or plague.

Views of Irish farming

Arable farming was hard work for people living on the land. They had to plough it, sow the seed and harvest the crops with sickles. After that, they threshed the grain with flails until the seeds fell out. Pastoral farming was much less hard work, so it was seen as a sign of a lazy man or an uncivilised country. Most English farming was arable and English writers sometimes scorned the Irish for being too idle to cultivate land for crops. These English writers helped to build up a picture of Ireland as only a pastoral country, but was this true?

B A description of Irish farming

The writer is a half-English, half-Welsh supporter of the Norman invasion of Ireland:

"[The Irish] live on beasts only, and live like beasts. They have not progressed at all from the primitive habits of pastoral living . . . They use the fields generally as pasture, but pasture in poor condition. Little is cultivated, and even less sown . . . The wealth of the soil is lost, not through the fault of the soil, but because there are no farmers to cultivate even the best land."

(From Gerald the Welshman, *The Topography of Ireland*, 1188)

C A modern historian's findings

4 *What may have made Gerald write what he did?*

5 *What kinds of evidence does the modern historian use to disagree with Gerald?*

"Cereal growing was both an extensive and an important activity. Between 536 and 825, on five occasions, the annals record the loss of the corn crop due to unfavourable weather conditions. On two of these occasions at least, a famine resulted. Again and again between 800 and 1160, the annals record as a serious mishap the loss of part or all of the corn crop, due to wet or windy weather."

(From Donncha Ó Corráin, *Ireland Before the Normans*, 1972)

Are any countries in the world today as badly off as Ireland was a thousand years ago? Which are they? What sort of farming methods do the people use?

---

7 A land of many kings?

Many of the countries that make up Europe today have not existed in their present form for very long. So the political map of Europe was very different in the past. What about the political map of Ireland? Did Ireland exist as a country a thousand and more years ago? Was there a king of Ireland?

Kings, great-kings and province-kings

Until recent times, kings ran their kingdoms without much interference from anyone else – except more powerful kings, that is! This was true of Ireland long ago. The Brehon law-books describe three grades of kings. At the bottom of the scale was the king of a small local kingdom or *túath*. Then came the 'overking' who was king over several of these petty kings. And finally there was the 'king of overkings', who ruled a whole province.

The province-kings were the ones who mattered most. The kings under them gradually became less and less important. In the end they were no longer called king (*rí*) at all, but just *taoiseach* ('leader') or *tiarna* ('lord').

A The province-kingdoms of Ireland around AD 800

1   *Can you see a connection between any of these names and present-day names?*

Kings and the Church

Early societies needed people to care for the sick, to provide education and to lay down rules for behaviour. Some of this work was carried out by the Church, so that its leaders and the kings believed they needed to be in partnership. The Church preached obedience to the kings in earthly matters such as respect for the law, while the kings protected the Church and saw to it that their subjects paid church-taxes. The Irish Church taught that kings were appointed by God and showed this by consecrating them in a religious ceremony. In later years the Church consecrated kings in many countries in Europe but it seems that the practice started in Ireland.

B Accounts from the *Annals*

2 *Find Mumu, the Northern Uí Néill, and Ulaid on the map.*

3 *What do these two events tell us about the relationship between kings and the Church?*

"793 AD The church-tax of St Ailbe [of Emly] was levied in Mumu [Munster] and Artri son of Cathal was ordained king of Munster."

809 AD Dúnchú, the head of the church of Tullyish [Co. Down], was killed beside the shrine of St Patrick in the abbot's house . . . Aed son of Niall [king of the Northern Uí Néill] invaded Ulaid in revenge for the insult to St Patrick's shrine . . . "

(From the *Annals of Ulster*)

Was Ireland a 'country'?

About 630 an Irish poet called Senchán Torpéist suggested that all Irish people were descended from one man, Míl or Milesius of Spain. Later scholars added their own ideas about where the Irish had come from. They believed that the Irish were a separate nation and that Ireland was a separate country. The Brehon laws taught that things should be done 'according to the custom of the island of Ireland'. The best reason the writers had for the belief that the Irish were one nation was that they all spoke the same language.

Was there a high-kingship?

As we have seen, there were separate kings over each province, just as countries all over Europe were divided among kings and lords. But the idea grew that in the past Ireland had one king, one set of laws and one capital. This was a myth but it suited any province-king trying to make himself high-king or ruler over the other provinces.

Usually the most powerful province-kings were the Uí Néill. The map shows that their lands included the hill of Tara and Uí Néill supporters claimed that this was the ancient capital of Ireland. Many people believed this, and so being king of Tara helped the Uí Néill province-kings in their search for more power. One of their strongest kings was Máel Sechnaill I, and when he died in 862 the *Annals* called him 'king of all Ireland'. Later, other kings won enough power (mostly by fighting) to claim this title. But no 'king of all Ireland' held on to the high-kingship of the whole country for long before the other province-kings united to cut down his power.

1 *Explain the differences between the various kinds of kings found in Ireland in the seventh and eighth centuries.*

2 *Why do you think Senchán Torpéist wanted Irish people to believe that they were all descended from Milesius?*

8 Early Irish politics: Murder and mayhem?

Like many European countries until fairly recent times, early medieval Ireland was a very violent place. The books of *Annals* are our main way of finding out about the politics of the period and they are full of accounts of battles and murders. But what was all the fighting for? What were early Irish politics really about?

Violence and political power

Most people in Ireland in early medieval times were simple farmers who spent their lives peacefully, working on the land. Only small numbers lived as fighters and warriors. But the writers of the *Annals* concentrated on the lives of kings and warriors, and they were the people who did most of the fighting.

Nowadays, most people believe that violence is the wrong way to try to solve problems, but in early Ireland men were admired for their bravery in battle and skill in the use of arms.

We talk of political leaders being elected to power and falling from power. In the past, power was not held by politicians but by kings. Kings sometimes did rise to power by being elected – that is, by being chosen to take the place of a previous king. But they often fell from power on the battlefield.

There was no definite rule for choosing a king. In any kingdom (whether it was a tiny *túath* or a whole province), a man might make himself king as long as he was brave enough, popular enough and powerful enough. If he was the son or close relative of a previous king, his chances were better.

But kings often had several wives and many sons by each. In a short time a royal family was divided into three or more rival branches, with cousins and second-cousins all trying to push the others out and make their leader king. If they did not manage to do so, they might invade the lands of another tribe and set up as kings there. You can see how this worked in Connacht around the eighth century.

According to legend, the Uí Fiachrach were all descended from one man called Fiachra. But the family split up into two main branches who fought with each other. The Uí Fiachrach Muaide branch ended up in north-west Connacht, and the Uí Fiachrach Aidni ended up in the south of the province. However, the descendants of Fiachra were not only fighting themselves. They faced competition for control of Connacht from another dynasty. These were the Uí Briúin, all said to be descended from a man called Brión. About the year 700, the Uí Briúin were based around Carnfree in County Roscommon. Over the years, they too began to split. The first branch, the Uí Briúin Aí, stayed in the original homelands. As they grew they also produced new branches, and the most famous of them were the O'Connors.

A A ninth-century warrior

(From the *Book of Kells*)

1 *What sort of man do you think the painter was trying to show?*

B Connacht in the eighth century

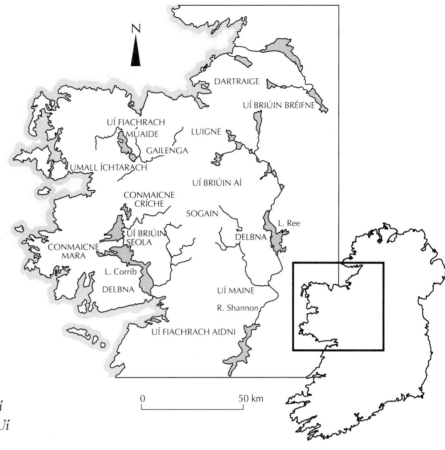

2 *Find two branches of the Uí Fiachrach and three of the Uí Briúin.*

The second wing of the Uí Briúin were the Uí Briúin Seola, who were pushed out by the others and settled in new lands east of Lough Corrib. They later split up again and the famous O'Flaherty family were their most successful branch. Finally, there was the Uí Briúin Bréifne, who moved north-east, kicked out other weaker tribes from their lands in Cavan and Leitrim, and set themselves up as kings there. Later, their chief family was the O'Rourkes.

And so it went on over the centuries, one family rising in power, another falling. That is what most of the fighting was about. As families grew, they made war on their distant relatives to try to grab the kingship and they spread out into the lands of other tribes. Not everyone can be a winner, however, and in time many families faded out. Like the lesser kings they fell down the social ladder and let others compete for the top prize of the kingship of Connacht.

*In 1911 an Irish historian called G.H. Opren wrote that the politics of early Ireland was a 'maze of inter-provincial and inter-tribal fighting' (*Ireland under the Normans 1, 39*). What did he mean? What made him see the struggles for power in this way? If you were writing about those times how would you explain the politics?*

9 How did Ulster fit in?

Perhaps the most powerful province in Ireland in those early times was Ulster. Its capital, Emain Macha, was a place of special importance, and the early Christians built a church nearby at Armagh which became the most important one in the whole island. How does Ulster fit into the jigsaw puzzle of early Ireland? What connection did it have with Scotland?

Emain Macha

In the time before Christianity arrived, Emain Macha was probably the most important place in Ireland. It was the capital of Ulster, the strongest of all the Irish kingdoms. The people of Ulster were called the Ulaid and the word 'Ulster' comes from *Ulaid's tír* ('the Ulaid's land'). To hold on to their land the Ulaid had to fight.

This is the background to the greatest Irish saga, the *Táin Bó Cúailgne* (The Cattle-raid of Cooley). It tells us about the reign in Emain Macha of King Conor mac Nessa, and about Queen Maeve of Cruachu, the capital of Connacht. It describes a war between Connacht and Ulster, and the noble deeds of Cú Chulainn, the champion of Ulster.

A Emain Macha (Navan Fort, near Armagh city) a few years ago

1 *Next to the remains of Emain Macha is a limestone quarry which threatened to destroy the site. In 1986, at the last minute, the quarrying was stopped by government order. Explain whether or not you think it was right to stop the quarrying.*

The rise of the Uí Néill

By the middle of the fifth century, the kingdom ruled from Emain Macha had fallen. The man who conquered it was probably Niall of the Nine Hostages, who ruled the midlands of Ireland from his capital at Tara.

The family of Niall of the Nine Hostages were called the Uí Néill. Legend has it that some of Niall's sons settled down in the north-west of Ulster. One of them, Conall, gave his name to Tír Conaill (now Donegal) while the name of another, Eóghan, is found in Inis Eóghain (or the Inishowen peninsula). Later, descendants of Eóghan spread south and gave their name to Tír Eóghain (or Tyrone).

As the power of the Uí Néill spread, the Ulaid were forced to move east across the River Bann into Antrim and Down. They ruled here for many centuries and their place in mid-Ulster was taken by the kingdom of Airgialla (see the map on page 16).

The Dál Riada and Scotland

The kings of the Ulaid ruled over many smaller local kingdoms. One was the Dál Riada, who lived in the Glens of Antrim. About the time the Emain Macha fell, the people of Dál Riada sailed over to Argyll in Scotland. They conquered land in Argyll and then moved out into the Hebrides and over much of the Highlands. In the ninth century the most famous Dál Riada king, Kenneth mac Alpin, became the first king of a united Scotland.

The Dál Riada brought the Irish language with them to Argyll. This language still survives today as Scottish Gaelic and is spoken by thousands of people today in the west of Scotland.

A Latin word used by the Romans for Ireland was *Scotia*, and they called the Irish *Scoti*. When the Dál Riada went from Antrim to Argyll they were, of course, looked on as Irish or *Scoti*. So when they conquered that country for themselves the name *Scotia* stuck to it. Gradually people began to use another Latin name, *Hibernia*, for Ireland, and Scotland was born. But the original Scots were Irishmen from Ulster!

B Ireland and Scotland

2 *Is what Gerald wrote eight hundred years ago still true? Can you think of any things that Scotland and Ireland have in common today?*

"The northern part of Britain is also called Scotia because it is known to be lived in by people who were originally from Ireland. To this day, the closeness in language and culture . . . and customs bears out this ."

(From Gerald the Welshman, *The Topography of Ireland*, 1188)

In the seventeenth century, many thousands of Scottish people came to settle in Ulster and their Ulster-Scots descendants are still very numerous there to this day. But, who knows, the ancestors of some of them may have been the Dál Riada who went from Ulster to Scotland over fifteen hundred years ago!

The ancestors of many people in Ulster today came there only three or four hundred years ago. Emain Macha was built over a thousand years before that. Who should take pride in this very important archaeological site? Everybody, or just people whose ancestors were in Ireland at the time it was built?

10 How were Ireland and Britain linked?

Britain and Ireland lie so close to each other that it is understandable that Ireland should have closer contacts with Britain than anywhere else. In the 800 or so years since the Normans invaded, Britain and Ireland have often quarrelled. What was the situation like before the Normans arrived?

Church contacts

Every year on 17 March many people all over the world become Irish for a day, but the man whose feast day they celebrate – St Patrick – was British! Changes sometimes reach Ireland slowly because it lies on the edge of Europe. Those changes have often come through contacts with Britain. So it was with Christianity. Most of the first missionaries who came to Ireland were from Britain, and the Irish Church owes them a great debt.

Later, the Irish repaid the favour. Many famous Irish churchmen, such as St Aidan of Lindisfarne, went to Britain to preach the Gospel. They built up churches and monasteries and converted many to Christianity. By then Ireland was famous as a place of learning and British monks and priests came to Ireland to study. In this way, the people of both islands got to know each other better.

Goods and people

There were other ways in which the Irish and British had contact with each other. Then, as now, there were strong trading links between the two countries. The Irish were big importers of goods like iron and salt and thought highly of British horses. In return, they exported animal hides, leather, wool and clothing made from them.

The ugliest side of trading was dealing in slaves which the Irish had carried on from earliest times. Some traders raided Britain to capture slaves and bring them back to Ireland for sale. Others bought them from greedy merchants who sold slaves. St Patrick himself was brought to Ireland as a slave while still a boy. At the same time as British slaves were being brought to Ireland, there were poor Irish people who were forced to emigrate to Britain in search of work.

A One reason for the Norman invasion

1 *What sin had the Irish committed? What did Gerald think was the punishment for it?*

Gerald the Welshman gives a reason why God permitted the Normans to invade Ireland:

" . . . this disaster struck [the Irish] by the stern judgement of God's vengeance. It had once been their habit to buy Englishmen from merchants as well as from robbers and pirates, and to make slaves of them, but now they in turn would be turned into slaves by that same race."

(From Gerald the Welshman, *The Conquest of Ireland*, 1189)

B St Cadoc builds a church in Wales in the sixth century

2 *What information about Laoire's life can you find here?*

"And it happened that a certain Irishman named Laoire, a stranger, but a skilful builder, being forced by poverty, came to him with his children, so that by the practice of his skill he might obtain food for himself and his family."

(From *Life of St Cadoc*, written in the twelfth century)

C Irish influence and Ogam stones

3 *Who were the Irish who settled in western Scotland?*

4 *How does the map help to show where the settlers in Wales and Cornwall came from?*

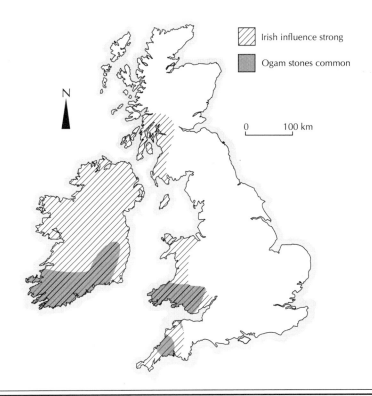

Irish influence strong

Ogam stones common

N

0   100 km

Irish colonies in Britain

Irish people have often complained about British interference in Ireland but in early times it was sometimes the other way round. Around the fourth century Irish people set up small colonies in south-west and north Wales, and in Devon and Cornwall in England. These settlements gradually died out but they were followed by the very successful Irish colony which the Dál Riada set up in western Scotland.

The Irish in Wales may have left one curious legacy. In the Irish language, the word for an Irishman is *Gael*. It seems that this comes from the Welsh word used to describe these Irish invaders, *Gwyddel*, which probably meant 'wild man'! When the Normans invaded Ireland in the late twelfth century many of the fighters and farmers who came with them were Welsh. For all we know, some of these may have been the descendants of Irishmen who invaded Wales five or six centuries earlier!

1 *In the 1130s, an English writer called William of Malmesbury asked: 'Of what value would Ireland be if deprived of the merchandise of England?' What did he mean? Is this still true today?*

2 *How is William of Malmesbury's view one-sided? List the examples in this Unit of Irish contributions to life in Britain.*

11 Armagh: Headquarters of the Church?

Armagh is still the centre of both the Roman Catholic and the main Protestant Church in Ireland. How long has this been the case?

Armagh stakes its claim

The official title of the archbishop of Armagh in Irish is *Comharba Phádraig*, 'the successor of Patrick'. St Patrick has a special link with Armagh because he probably built a church there in the fifth century. Two hundred years later the bishop and priests at Armagh were trying to make it one of the chief churches in the country. To build up Armagh's position it was important to show everyone that it was special to Patrick. So the church leaders at Armagh wrote the *Book of the Angel*. It tells how an angel told Patrick that Armagh would be set up by God as a great church over a vast area because Patrick 'loved Armagh above all the lands of the Irish'.

About 670 a bishop called Tírechán wrote a book describing Patrick's journeys and listing the churches he started. This helped to convince people that Patrick did set up all these churches and that they all now belonged to Armagh and should pay their church-taxes to it. Church leaders began to recognise Armagh's special place. In 640 Pope John IV wrote to a list of Irish church leaders and put the bishop of Armagh at the head. Later in the seventh century a bishop from Laois agreed that the bishop of Armagh was his superior and others began to do the same.

A Armagh's claim

1 *Which 'city' is the* Book of the Angel *about?*

2 *Who is the 'successor of Patrick' in Tírechán's* Memoir?

3 *How do these extracts tell us that Armagh was trying to make itself the leading church in Ireland?*

A1 "This city has been made by God supreme and free, and has been specially chosen by the angel of God, and by the holy, apostolic man, Bishop Patrick . . . it stands above all the churches and all the monasteries of Ireland."

(From the *Book of the Angel*, seventh century)

A2 " The deserters, robbers and warlords of Ireland hate Patrick's church possessions. They have taken away from him what was his, and are afraid, because if the 'successor of Patrick' were to look for what belongs to him, he could get almost the whole island."

(From Tírechán's *Memoir*, AD 670)

Around the year 690 another Armagh writer called Muirchú wrote the *Life-story of St Patrick*. He tells of Patrick lighting the Easter fire at Tara, a story about the saint's victory over the pagan druids. Tara was the capital of the Uí Néill and so it was very useful for Armagh to keep on friendly terms with their kings. They could protect the Church with their armies and share some of their wealth with it.

Armagh and the Uí Néill

In this way, as the Uí Néill grew stronger, so did the bishops of Armagh. A special tomb was built at Armagh where Uí Néill kings were buried. In 1014 the greatest of all the kings of Ireland, Brian Boru, was also buried in the 'mausoleum of the kings'.

Gradually the bishops of Armagh were accepted as head of the Irish Church. They were able to send officials around the country to collect their taxes and enforce their law, called the 'Law of Patrick'.

The priests kept a famous book called, the *Canóin Phádraig* ('St Patrick's Canon') which is now called the *Book of Armagh* and can be seen in Trinity College, Dublin. It was written in Armagh in 807 and has copies of the books about Patrick which you read about on the page opposite. Another precious relic at Armagh was St Patrick's bell. Around the year 1100, craftsmen at Armagh made a beautiful shrine to hold it which still exists in the National Museum in Dublin.

B The Shrine of St Patrick's Bell

4   *What does the Shrine tell us about the wealth of Armagh, the skills of its craftsmen and the high regard for St Patrick?*

In 1152, the Pope set up four archdioceses in Ireland, at Armagh, Cashel, Dublin and Tuam, with the archbishop of Armagh as the head. Eventually, Dublin's archbishop became known as the 'Primate of Ireland' but the archbishop of Armagh was 'Primate of ALL Ireland'. We still use both titles today.

1   *'What reasons have we for calling Armagh 'the see of Saint Patrick'?*

2   *We cannot say for certain that St Patrick did set up Armagh, but it has been seen as his special church for over thirteen hundred years. Should this continue?*

12 Why were monasteries so important?

Ireland stood out from most other places in Western Europe because its most important churches were run by monks or nuns in monasteries which they built all over the country. Why was this? What sort of life did the monks and nuns lead in an early Irish monastery?

Why did people build monasteries?

Some of those who set up monasteries in Ireland began their religious life in British monasteries. There they became convinced that the monastic life was the best way of serving God. St Enda studied in a monastery in Galloway in Scotland. He returned to Ireland and set up his own monastery on Inis Mór, the largest of the Aran Islands. It was a wild, lonely place but many Irish abbots received their training here before they went off to rule their own monasteries.

St Finnian studied in St Cadoc's monastery in Wales. Later he set up a monastery at Clonard. It became one of Ireland's greatest monastic schools and won Finnian the title 'teacher of the saints of Ireland'. Among his pupils were Colum Cille, Ciarán, Colmán and Brendan.

A A monastery built on rock

1 *Why do you think Enda chose the rocky island?*

When St Enda built his monastery on Inis Mór, the king of Munster is said to have asked:

"That place is all rock. I promised Saint Patrick a gift of land for the Church, but it was to be the best land in the kingdom. Why go to Aran, you can have much better land near Cashel?"

(From the *Life-story of St Enda,* written in the twelfth century)

Another reason for monasteries being so popular might be the epidemic of plague which swept through Ireland in the 540s. It killed many people, including Saints Ciarán of Clonmacnoise, Finnian of Clonard, and Mobhí of Glasnevin. Fear of its awful effects must have caused many people to look to God for help or forgiveness. One way of doing this could have been to become a monk. Kings and lords may also have decided that God would be pleased if they gave land to start a monastery.

B Skellig Michael

Skellig Michael is on a rock about twelve kilometres off the Kerry coast. Monks first lived in the beehive cells more than a thousand years ago.

2 *Why do you think Irish monks chose to go to such a place? What does it tell us about them?*

Many monasteries were built on fertile land but even there monks usually preferred to live on their own in tiny cold and damp 'cells'. In other countries they would have lived together in communal houses and dormitories.

St Columbanus made a rule that monks should 'pray daily, fast daily, study daily, work daily'. His *Rule* sums up the lives of most monks. They had several hours' prayer each day in the little monastic church. They went without food until the late afternoon every Wednesday and Friday, and in Lent they fasted every day (except Sunday) until evening and were then only allowed a light meal. The Irish monks copied manuscripts and studied the Scriptures. Some were expert in the Latin books of famous Roman writers such as Virgil.

Monasteries were also places where the homeless or sick could often find a refuge. The monastery at Lismore had a colony for lepers, who were usually driven out of their homes. Travellers could spend a night or two in a monastery's guest house. Many monasteries ran schools where young men studied for the priesthood and, perhaps, where future royal officials received part of their training. Some of the schools gave advanced courses and did the work of present-day universities.

Some monks did the manual work such as sowing and harvesting, fishing and bee-keeping, but very often the work on the monastery's estates was done by laymen who lived there with their wives and children, making some monasteries into a kind of village community.

C The monastery at Kells

3 *Describe what you see in the picture. Can you find where the lay workers would have lived?*

4 *Do you think it was a wealthy monastery? Explain your answer.*

5 *Why do you think it needed walls around it?*

(A sketch of what the monastery at Kells, County Meath, might have looked like about AD 1100)

Most of the monasteries' founders were from the aristocracy, like Colum Cille who was related to the kings of the Donegal area. He founded Iona, and ten out of its first twelve abbots came from that same family. They looked on their monasteries almost as family property and later on abbots often married and were succeeded by their sons. By the eighth century or so, the monasteries in Ireland had risen to a position of great wealth and power. Sometimes, they even went to war with each other!

D Two communities at war

6   *What does this account tell us about the activities and the size of some Irish monasteries in the eighth century?*

"764 AD . . . The battle of Argaman took place between the monastic community of Clonmacnoise and the monastic community of Durrow . . . Two hundred of the community of Durrow were killed."

(From the *Annals of Ulster*)

Such fighting was part of the Irish way of life and monasteries could not help becoming part of it. However, there were many Irish men and women who continued to devote their lives to God. The fame of their holiness spread because they went abroad as 'pilgrims for Christ', preaching the Gospel, and starting monasteries and schools all over Britain and Europe.

We can often trace the places where there were early Irish monasteries and churches from place names:

Cill means a monk's dwelling or a small monastic church. You find it in place-names beginning with Kil(l) and it is extremely common.

Díseart (as in Desertmartin, County Derry) means 'a hermitage'.

Domhnach (as in Donaghmore, Donaghpatrick, etc.) means a 'large church'.

Where is the nearest such place to you? How did it get its name?

13 Why did Iona become important?

Iona is a tiny island off the west coast of Scotland. Yet it has an important place in Irish history. What gave it such importance? Iona also helped to bring about great religious and political changes in Scotland and northern England. How did this happen?

Colum Cille

Ireland's first great missionary was St Colum Cille. His name means 'the dove of the church' and he is often called Columba, which is the Latin for dove. He was born into a famous royal family in 521 at Gartan, County Donegal. His great-grandfather is said to have been Niall of the Nine Hostages. So Colum Cille might have become king of the Northern Uí Néill but instead he decided to join the Church. Tradition has it that he founded his first monastery at Derry at the age of twenty-five. He also set up other monasteries such as Durrow, County Laois. In 563 Colum Cille decided to leave Ireland for Iona, taking with him twelve companions, like Jesus's twelve disciples.

Iona was on the edge of Dál Riada, the part of Scotland that had been settled by Irish people. Missionaries had already visited Dál Riada but the Christian faith was not firmly established there. To the north of Dál Riada lived their enemies, the Picts. Three years before Colum Cille arrived in Iona the Picts defeated Dál Riada and weakened their power in Scotland.

Colum Cille and his band of monks worked hard to strengthen the position of the Christian Church in Dál Riada. They travelled in tiny currachs to preach to the people who lived in the settlements along the shores and estuaries.

A Iona in the sixth and seventh centuries

1 *Find Iona on the map. Why do you think Colum Cille chose to go there?*

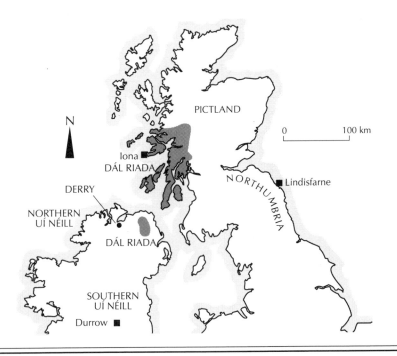

Colum Cille also played a big part in making Dál Riada into a stronger kingdom. He persuaded the Scots to agree to a new king, Aedán mac Gabráin. According to tradition, Aedán then went to Iona where Colum Cille anointed him. As far as we can tell, this is the first time in Europe that a churchman performed the ceremony to make someone king. The abbots of Iona became the primates of Dál Riada because of the great work done by Colum Cille and the support he gave to the king. In time, Dál Riada grew to become the kingdom of Scotland and for centuries Iona was its most important church, where its kings were buried.

Dál Riada was already partly Christian when Colum Cille went to Iona, but the kingdom of the Picts was still pagan. Colum Cille visited the king of Pictland and made peace between the Picts and Dál Riada. He also got permission for his monks to travel safely as far as the Orkney islands to preach the faith. This was the start of the spread of Christianity through the whole of Scotland.

Aidan of Lindisfarne

Not long after Colum Cille's death in 597, monks from Iona took the lead in spreading Christianity into Northumbria. This was a pagan kingdom set up in the fifth century by Anglo-Saxons who invaded Britain from Germany. Early in the seventh century, the king of Northumbria was killed in battle and his son Oswald fled to Scotland. There, he became a Christian. In 634 Oswald won back his kingdom and he invited the holy men of Iona to join him.

The man who led the Iona missionaries was the Irish saint, Bishop Aidan. He set up his headquarters at Lindisfarne, a little island just off the coast. Aidan spoke no English, but Oswald could speak Irish and so acted as his interpreter. For over sixteen years Aidan preached, and founded churches and monasteries all over Northumbria.

B **An English monk's account of the Irish missionaries in Northumbria**

2   *Find four activities of Irish monks in this story.*

3   *The monks from Lindisfarne organised the Church in a similar way to the Church in Ireland. How?*

"Then many Irish arrived day by day in Britain and proclaimed the word of God with great devotion in all the province under King Oswald's rule, and their priests gave the grace of baptism to those who believed. Churches were built in several places, and the people flocked gladly to hear the word of God, while the king gave lands and property to set up monasteries, and the English, both noble and poor, were taught by their Irish teachers to follow a monastic life."

(From Bede, *The Ecclesiastical History*, AD 731)

Annals and manuscripts

Iona became the centre of a network of monasteries which spread across Ireland, Scotland, and Northumbria. Its monks and abbots helped to make kings and arranged treaties between different kingdoms. In this way they came to know a great deal about what was going on in the world outside their monastery. So it is not surprising that they began to record the important events of each year in the books we call *Annals*. The Irish *Annals* give us a lot of information about the times and it seems the first ones were put together at Iona.

The group of monasteries connected with Colum Cille and Iona also became one of the great European centres for art. In these houses the monks copied and created many beautiful hand-written books, or manuscripts. By looking carefully at these two pictures you can see how Iona helped to enrich the work of Irish monks.

The *Cathach* of Colum Cille is the oldest book in Ireland. It is a little book of Psalms that was possibly copied out before Colum Cille died in 597. Tradition has it that Colum Cille himself wrote it but it may have been the work of one of his monks. Seventy or eighty years later a monk in another of Colum Cille's monasteries copied out the Gospels. We call his book the *Book of Durrow* because it was kept for many years at the monastery there. The picture shows a carpet-page from it. The twisting-animal designs were borrowed from the Anglo-Saxons by monks connected with Colum Cille's monasteries.

C The *Cathach* and the *Book of Durrow*

4 *Compare the designs at the capital letter in the* Cathach *with the designs on the* Book of Durrow. *How are they similar and different?*

5 *In the* Book of Durrow *what can you see in a) the outer designs and b) the inner circle?*

6 *Where had the monks of Iona travelled at the time of a) the* Cathach *and b) the* Book of Durrow?

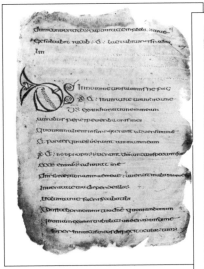

1 *There are several reasons for the importance of Iona which you have read about. Explain which you think is the most important.*

2 *Look again at Iona on the map. Make a list of the advantages and disadvantages of it being located where it is.*

3 *For centuries, people responded to the* Cathach *as a most sacred relic. The O'Donnells of Tir Connel carried it into battle, hoping it would bring them victory. Why did they think it was so special?*

14 An island of saints?

Even before Colum Cille died, other monks were leaving Ireland for Europe. Why was there a need for them in Europe in the seventh and eighth centuries? Their achievements gave Ireland the reputation of being an island of saints. When did people begin to think of Ireland in this way? Was the reputation deserved?

The Dark Ages

In the fourth and fifth century Europe was invaded by peoples who were not Christian. These pagan invaders caused the Roman Empire to collapse. They settled on the land and ignored the towns where Roman officials had their headquarters. As the towns fell into ruins, so did the early Christian churches and schools. It seemed there was only one way for Christianity to survive and for Europe to keep alive a knowledge of books and the Latin and Greek languages. Men of faith and learning must become monks. An Italian saint called Benedict took the lead in the 520s when he set up his famous hilltop monastery at Monte Cassino in Italy.

The monasteries in Ireland were also becoming well established and soon Irish missionaries left to play an important part in rebuilding a network of centres of Christian faith and learning throughout Europe. We call this Ireland's 'Golden Age' because it was the time when Ireland made its greatest contribution to the civilisation of Europe. It showed itself in great learning, in beautiful works of art, in the holiness of its saints.

Columbanus

Columbanus stands out for his contribution to Europe's Christian recovery. He spent many years studying under St Comgall at Bangor, a famous monastic centre of learning on Belfast Lough. He became famous as a teacher but he told Comgall that he desired to abandon his homeland and become a 'pilgrim for Christ'.

In 591, Columbanus set off for France with twelve companions (just as Colum Cille had when he sailed to Iona). In France, the practice of Christianity had almost collapsed. Columbanus went to the king of Burgundy, who was so impressed by his preaching that he asked him to stay. The saint built his first monastery at Annegray, on the ruins of a Roman fort that Attila the Hun (one of the invaders) had destroyed.

At Annegray, Columbanus lived at first on herbs, roots and the bark of trees. He began to attract followers and soon they needed a new monastery. They built it at Luxeuil, a few kilometres away. It became very important because many monks who set up their own monasteries were trained there. Within a generation, France was dotted with new monasteries. In the seventh century alone, about 300 were founded in France. St Columbanus himself set up others called daughters of the mother-house, Luxeuil, and he wrote his famous *Rule*, explaining how their monks should live.

He insisted on silence, prayer and fasting, to be broken only by light evening meals of porridge, vegetables or bread, with only water to drink. Above all else, he was a scholar and his writings had a great influence on the Church throughout Western Europe. He and St Benedict, who also wrote a famous *Rule* for his monks, are known as 'the founders of Western monasticism'.

A An Irish monk's prayer-book and its satchel

1 *Wherever Irish monks went abroad they carried books with them in their leather satchels. These were their most treasured possessions. Why?*

Eventually Columbanus was forced to leave France. He and his companions rowed up the River Rhine to Lake Constance. Even though he was in his seventies, Columbanus headed for Italy, where he founded his last monastery, at Bobbio in 612, and there he died three years later.

B Memories of Irish monks in Europe

2 *St Bernard was a Frenchman. How long had Columbanus been dead when he wrote about him? What does this tell us?*

"[Bangor] . . . produced many thousands of monks, and was the head of many monasteries. A truly holy place it was and full of saints, bringing forth most abundant fruit to God . . . Swarms of saints poured forth [from it] into foreign lands as though a flood had risen. One of them, Columbanus, came to our France, and built the monastery of Luxeuil, and made there a great community . . . "

(From Bernard of Clairvaux, *The Life-story of St Malachy*, written in 1149)

Gall and Fursa

One of Columbanus's twelve followers from Bangor was a monk called Gall. When Columbanus went off to Bobbio, Gall decided to stay in Switzerland, which was still mostly pagan. At first he lived as a hermit. Then Gall began to preach and soon gathered a small group of disciples. He spent the rest of his life there and has been called 'the apostle of Switzerland'. The Swiss city of St Gallen still bears his name.

Many exiled Irish monks and scholars visited his monastery. So its library gathered a large collection of the manuscripts which they brought from Ireland. Nearly all the books that were left in Ireland at this time have been lost, but the St Gallen library has preserved many of these priceless Irish manuscripts to the present day.

Hundreds of other Irishmen preached the Gospel in Europe at that time. St Fursa was an Irish abbot who went to East Anglia in England in 633. The local king had become a Christian and wanted to spread the faith among his people. St Fursa set up a monastery at Burgh Castle and spent over twelve years preaching and converting. Fursa and his two brothers then went to the Continent and did much to revive Christianity in northern France and Belgium. When Fursa died his body was brought to Péronne in France and a colony of Irish pilgrims grew around his tomb. The city came to be called 'Péronne of the Irish'.

C Bede tells us about St Fursa

3 *Why did Fursa become an exile, according to Bede?*

4 *What was it about him that made people want to become Christians?*

"There came from Ireland a holy man named Fursa, famous for his words and doings and outstanding in virtue. His purpose was to spend his life as a pilgrim for love or our Lord . . . Inspired by the example of his goodness and the effectiveness of his teaching, many unbelievers were converted to Christ . . ."

(From Bede, *The Ecclesiastical History*, AD 731)

D Irish monasteries in Europe in the seventh century

5 *Many of the monasteries are near rivers and lakes. Why?*

6 *How do you think the monks travelled from Ireland?*

7 *In which modern countries are the monasteries? Are any of these places still important today?*

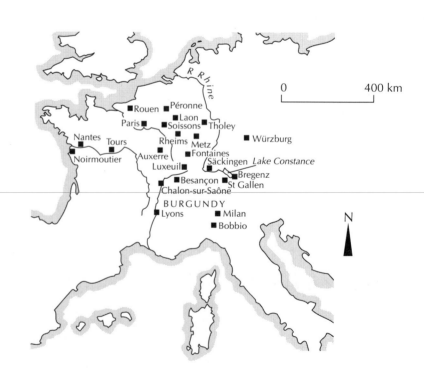

An island of saints

People throughout Europe met these Irish monks and saw them as saints and holy men. An Irish monk in Germany in the thirteenth century was so proud of these early Irish exiles that he said of them: 'The sick, both men and women, recovered health by touching their garments, or merely through their blessing, and in response to their prayers the dead were raised to life'. He was exaggerating but what he meant was that people all over Europe thought that there was something especially holy about the Irish monks.

As Irish monasteries grew, so did the fame those who started them. After monks began to jot down events of each year in the *Annals*, it was only a matter of time before they wrote down the life-story of the saints who founded their monasteries. The oldest of these books is the *Life-story of St Brigid*, by Cogitosus. Then, in 643 Jonas, an Italian monk who lived in the monastery at Bobbio, wrote a book about St Columbanus. He told his readers that 'the race of the Irish, though under different laws from those of other nations, are yet so strong in their Christian beliefs, that they outdo all neighbouring nations in faith'. Altogether, we still have about 150 lives of Irish saints written in Latin and Irish and they helped to spread their fame.

E Early mentions of the 'island of saints'

8 *Is the name 'island of saints' a modern invention?*

E1 "Ireland, the island of saints, is exceedingly full of very many holy men and miracles."

(From Marianus Scotus, *Chronicle*, written at Mainz in Germany in the 1070s)

E2 "After a short time, there was no deserted spot, almost no corner of land or place in the island, however remote, which was not filled up with holy monks and nuns, so that Ireland was quite rightly given throughout the world, the special name 'Island of Saints'."

(From the English monk Jocelin's *Life-story of St Patrick*, written in the 1180s)

---

1 *In 1185, an Irish monk at Regensburg wrote the* Life-story *of an abbot of the monastery, an Irishman called Marianus. He describes the pain of the Irish monks leaving behind 'the sweet earth of their native land . . . the green isle'. If it was so painful, why do you think so many Irish monks chose to go into exile?*

2 *What reasons would you give for Irish saints playing such an important part in European Christianity and learning?*

15 An island of scholars?

In Unit 4 we saw the flowering of learning that produced great epics like the *Táin* which were usually written in the Irish language. But another kind of learning won Ireland the name 'the island of scholars'. What sort of learning was it and why was it important? Who were these scholars and how did their fame spread?

A reputation for learning?

Ireland escaped the troubles of the Dark Ages and Christianity continued to grow there. Its many monasteries had schools where monks learned to read and write in Latin and Irish and studied the Bible and other holy books as well as famous Roman writings. Just when learning and scholarship were almost dying out in many other parts of Europe, the reputation of Ireland's schools started to spread.

A Going to Ireland to study

An Anglo-Saxon scholar, Aldhelm, complains about people going from Britain to study in Ireland:

"The wandering back and forth of those crossing the deep sea in ships is as busy as a swarm of bees . . . Why, I ask, is Ireland (where the crowds of students go by the fleet-load) raised up to such a privileged position, as if here in the fertile soil of Britain teachers could not be found?"

(From Aldhelm's letter to Heahfrith, written about 700)

B Bede writes about Irish teachers

1 *How do Bede and Aldhelm agree about Irish schools and teachers?*

2 *Do they give good evidence that Ireland was an island of scholars?*

"664 AD . . . At this time, there were many English nobles and common folk who had left their own land and gone to Ireland . . . some of these devoted themselves faithfully to the monastic life, while others preferred to travel around Ireland, to the cells of the various teachers, and to apply themselves to study. The Irish welcomed them all gladly, gave them their daily food, and also provided them with books to read, and with teaching, without asking for any payment."

(From Bede, *The Ecclesiastical History*, AD 731)

Irish scholars in Europe

The first powerful European ruler really to notice the Irish scholars was Charlemagne, who started to rule over most of France and Germany in 768. He saw the need to revive learning and summoned great scholars from other countries to teach throughout his lands. Charlemagne appointed one Irish scholar, Clement, as master of the school at his palace in Aachen and another, Dúngal, was sent as a teacher to Pavia in Italy.

The two most famous Irish scholars on the Continent at this time were Sedulius Scotus and John Scotus Eriugena. 'Scotus' means 'the Irishman' and 'Eriugena' means 'born of Ériu (or Ireland)'. Sedulius arrived at Liège in France about 848, and become professor of the school there. He was an all-round scholar who wrote several grammar-books, a work of philosophy, a book about the psalms, notes on St Paul's Letters and a handbook on princely behaviour. Like many Irishmen down the ages, Sedulius also wrote poetry and we still have over eighty of his fine Latin poems.

John Eriugena was a teacher at Laon, in the palace school of Charlemagne's grandson. In his day he was looked on as the greatest scholar in Europe. He also knew Greek, which had almost died out in Europe. Where he learned it we do not know, possibly in Ireland but perhaps only after he came to the continent.

There were other Irish scholars whose writing has survived. A book written about AD 800 by a schoolmaster from Kildare still exists in a monastery at Carinthia in Austria. It includes one of the oldest poems in the Irish language. The author describes what his work has in common with his white cat, Pangur Bán.

C The Irish £5 note, showing John Scotus Eriugena

3 *Why do you think John was picked to be shown?*

4 *If you had to choose someone's portrait for the note, whose would it be? Explain why.*

D Pangur Bán, the cat

5 *How does the scholar see the connection between his life and his cat?*

I and Pangur Bán my cat,
'Tis a like task we are at:
Hunting mice is his delight,
Hunting words I sit all night.

So in peace our tasks we ply,
Pangur Bán, my cat, and I.
In our arts we find our bliss,
I have mine and he has his.

Practice every day has made
Pangur perfect in his trade.
I get wisdom day and night
Turning darkness into light.

(Translated from the Irish by Robin Flower, *The Irish Tradition*, 1947)

What made scholars like Eriugena and Sedulius Scotus go off to the Continent? Had they different reasons from the missionaries like Columbanus and Fursa? Explain your answer.

16 Irish art: The work of angels?

One of the most exciting things about Ireland's 'Golden Age' is that we do not have to rely on history books alone to find out about it. We can see with our own eyes some of its finest achievements – its works of art. What is special about the art of the Golden Age?

The Book of Kells

Imagine you live in a time and place when you will only ever see three or four books in your entire life. Instead of flicking over the pages, you might spend a whole afternoon studying a page like the one below.

A **A portrait of St John in the *Book of Kells***

1 *Describe what you can see and what thoughts it leads to.*

2 *A leading expert has called it 'one of the greatest portraits of all time'. Give some reasons why he might think this.*

3 *On the cover of this book you can see a drawing of the arrest of Christ, also from the* Book of Kells. *In what ways are the pictures alike? Are any of the patterns repeated? Which do you prefer?*

B Gerald the Welshman describes a book in Kildare monastery

4 *When you looked at the page opposite, did you have the same first and second thoughts as Gerald?*

5 *Why do you think that Gerald thought it must have been the work of angels?*

"Of all the miracles of Kildare, none seems to me more miraculous than that wonderful book. . . It has the four Gospels, with almost as many drawings as pages, and all of them in marvellous colours . . . If you looked at them carelessly, you might think they were just rough drawings. But if you take the trouble to look very closely, and examine with your eyes the secrets of the art, you will notice such details, so delicate and subtle . . . that you will immediately say that all these things must have been the work, not of men, but of angels."

(From *The Topography of Ireland*, 1188)

Gerald was not fond of the Irish, and found it hard to believe that they could produce such a masterpiece. So, he decided that an angel must have created it! But in fact it was an Irish artist who did. Sad to say, like so many other treasures, the Kildare book has been lost but Gerald might just as well have been describing the *Book of Kells*.

In Unit 13 there is a picture of the oldest Irish manuscript book, the *Cathach* of Colum Cille, which is very plain. The *Book of Durrow* had more colour and decoration because Irish monks at Lindisfarne had come into contact with Anglo-Saxon art. The *Book of Kells* takes us a century further on.

By then, the network of Irish monasteries had spread into France, Germany and Italy. The Irish learned from the art of the Western Church based in Rome but they also came into contact with the Eastern or Byzantine Church, which had its headquarters in Constantinople (now Istanbul). Byzantine art was spreading from the east into western Europe at that time.

That is one reason why the *Book of Kells* is such a wonderful thing to look at. It has beautifully simple Irish patterns like the *Cathach*. It has the animals and decorations of the Anglo-Saxons, like those in the *Book of Durrow,* but it also has fascinating paintings of human figures which came from looking at Byzantine holy books. This great treasure-chest of ideas from all Europe reached Ireland because of the far-flung Irish monasteries.

Somewhere in Ireland or in the Irish monastery on Iona around 800 a group of monks took all these influences and turned them into this great book which still has something for people everywhere to admire. We do not know the names of the artists or for certain where they worked. All we know is that it was produced in one of the monasteries linked to Colum Cille. Kells was part of this family of monasteries and the *Book* was there in 1007 when it was stolen.

C Theft of the *Book of Kells*

6 *What does the second sentence tell you about how the* Book of Kells *was seen a thousand years ago?*

"The Great Gospel-book of Colum Cille was wickedly stolen at night from the west-sacristy of the great stone church of Kells. It was the most precious object of the Western World . . . This Gospel-book was recovered after two months and twenty nights, but its gold cover had been taken off it, and it was covered in turf."

(From the *Annals of Ulster*)

The monastic metalworkers

In 1867 a boy was digging potatoes on a rath in County Limerick when his spade turned up the object in the left of the picture below. In 1980, a man and his son digging for treasure on an old ruined monastery in County Tipperary came across the object on the right.

They are chalices, used for holding Communion wine. The first was made around 750. It is made of solid silver and has ornament of gold, copper, enamel and crystal. Today it is called the Ardagh Chalice. The second was made perhaps about 800. It is the Derrynaflan Chalice.

D The Ardagh and Derrynaflan chalices

7 *What differences can you spot between the two chalices?*

8 *What evidence can you see that these were made around the same time as the* Book of Kells?

If you visit the National Museum in Dublin or the Ulster Museum in Belfast, you will see other treasures such as ornamental covers for precious books, bishops' croziers and shrines for holding the relics of saints, like St Patrick's bell. All were made by craftsmen in the monastic workshops. Many more must have been lost over the centuries. They show how the Church could draw on ideas from the length and breadth of Europe. They are also evidence that the Church was wealthy. Much of its wealth was its own but some objects may have been given to the Church by rich people outside. We can see evidence of the wealth of Irish people in stories that have come down to us.

E An Irish noblewoman in an eighth-century story

9 *Make a list of the precious objects owned by the noblewoman in this story.*

10 *Supposing the story-writer knew of women like this, what can we learn about the wealth of Irish noble families in the eighth century?*

"He saw a woman at the well, and she had a silver comb with gold ornament. She was washing in a silver basin on which were four golden birds, and bright little purple gems on the outside. She wore a purple cloak of goose fleece, held with silver brooches engraved with gold, and a smock of green silk with gold embroidery. There were wonderful ornaments of animal design in gold and silver on her breast and shoulders."

(From *The Destruction of Da Derga's Hostel*)

Irish lords and their wives wore heavy woollen cloaks fastened together with brooches. Many of them still exist, and no two are the same. The finest of them all is one fit for a king and so has been named 'the Tara brooch' but it was actually found near the beach at Bettystown, County Meath, in 1850.

F The Tara brooch

11 *Why is this called the Tara brooch? Would it have been better to call it the Bettystown brooch?*

12 *Make a simple sketch to show how it was used.*

13 *Take one of the patterns and try to copy it.*

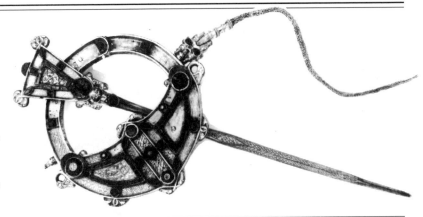

The art of the Golden Age has to be seen to be appreciated. Sometimes only when it is magnified can we see the astonishing beauty of the artist's illustration or the goldsmith's ornament. Irish art did not begin with the Golden Age and it certainly did not end with it. But never before or since have Ireland's artists been at the forefront of European art.

The Derrynaflan Chalice was discovered by people using a metal detector around a national monument; in other words, on a site that belongs to the entire nation. The state claimed it on behalf of the Irish people, to go into the National Museum. But the finders felt that they were entitled to keep it. Eventually, the Supreme Court in Dublin decided that the state was right.

Who do you think was right? Should the finders have been allowed to keep it? It is against the law for unqualified people to dig for treasure on important archaeological sites. Why do you think this is so?

17 The Vikings: Destroyers of a Golden Age?

In 795, Ireland was attacked for the first time by Vikings. Soon their raids became more frequent and many of them settled permanently in Ireland. Did their arrival bring the Golden Age to an end?

Sea and river raiders

The Vikings were bands of sea-warriors, mainly from Norway, who came west in search of plunder. Their excellent ships made it easy for them to travel great distances, attack their targets with lightning speed and then take to the high seas again. But they were not all just pirates. Some came to make new homes for themselves in Ireland and Britain.

The easiest targets of all were the monasteries on islands like Iona, Rathlin, Inishmurray and Inishbofin. Iona suffered a great deal and sixty-eight of the community were killed in one raid. As a result, in 807 its leaders decided to build a new monastery in Ireland, at Kells in County Meath. In 824, the Vikings even attacked the hermits on Skellig Michael and captured their Superior, so that he died of hunger and thirst.

A An Irish shrine

1 *How do you think the shrine got to Norway?*

2 *To the Irish, its contents were more important than the box itself. Why?*

3 *Which would be more valuable to the Vikings? Why?*

This shrine, to hold the relics of a saint, was made in Ireland about AD 800. It was found in a warrior's grave in Norway.

In the 830s the Vikings started to venture inland. In 832, they attacked Armagh three times in one month. By sailing up rivers like the Shannon, Boyne, Liffey and Erne they could attack the rich churches that had earlier been safe. They spent the whole winter of 840–41 on Lough Neagh and the following winter they built a camp in what was to become the city of Dublin.

B An Irish poem from a ninth-century manuscript

4 *Why can the monk afford to 'take his ease'?*

5 *Can we learn from this poem what Irish monks thought of the Vikings?*

6 *The book this poem is written in ended up in St Gallen in Switzerland. How do you think that happened?*

Fierce and wild is the wind tonight,

It tosses the tresses of the sea to white;

On such a night as this I take my ease;

Fierce Northmen only course the quiet seas.

(Translated by James Carney, in *Medieval Irish Lyrics*, 1967)

What were the effects of the Viking raids?

For a time it looked as though the Vikings would conquer the whole country. Instead they became part of everyday life, just one more violent group in a country that was already violent. Because monasteries and churches were rich, they were used to being attacked by armies, especially during a war or famine, when their large stocks of grain or cattle would come in very handy.

The Vikings did great damage to many monasteries but they did not actually destroy any. There were many rich churches around Dublin where they made their main base – such as Clondalkin, Crumlin, Glasnevin, Kilmainham, Lusk, Shankill, Swords and Tallaght. All survived.

However the Viking raids had bad effects on Irish art and learning. It may be that scholars like Eriugena and Sedulius, who went to the Continent in the ninth century, did so to escape from the Vikings. More and more students and teachers went to the schools of France and Germany. A French writer at this time says of Ireland 'almost the whole people, not caring about the dangers of the sea, are migrating with their many writers to our shores'.

Irish art suffered too. Craftsmen still turned out fine brooches for kings and nobles, but they seem to have had less work to do for the Church. The work they did do was not as fine as in the Golden Age. Perhaps some of the best craftsmen had been killed in the raids or perhaps there was no point in spending time and precious metal on a masterpiece that was going to be stolen The same is true of fine books. The Vikings were pagans and unable to read but they broke off the ornamental metal covers and threw the books away. Books were still put together in the monastic writing-rooms but it was expensive to illustrate one like the *Book of Kells* which took years of time and skill. So the standard of work dropped.

However, Irish craftsmen were helped by the fact that the Vikings set up trading towns around the coast. Traders brought silver from as far away as North Africa and craftsmen used this to make fine objects, especially pieces of jewellery like brooches. The form of art which improved most in the Viking age was sculpture. Stone lasts longer and cannot be carried off by attackers! This may explain why Irish churches began to build the High Crosses that are still standing after more than a thousand years. The earliest ones were built before the Vikings came but it was during the ninth century that they started to become real works of art and to show scenes from the Bible.

C High Cross of Moone, County Kildare

7 *Find Jesus on the Cross, Adam and Eve in the Garden, Abraham sitting on a chair about to sacrifice Isaac, and Daniel in the lions' den.*

8 *Why do you think this cross was made?*

1 *Make a list of 'good points' and 'bad points' about Ireland after the coming of the Vikings. Did they do more harm than good?*

2 *Write entries from a book of* Annals *for the years 795, 807, 824, 832. Use the style of language you can see in extracts from the* Annals *in this book.*

18 A war of Gaeil with Gaill?

Around the year 1100 a Munsterman wrote the history of Ireland from the coming of the Vikings to the Battle of Clontarf in 1014. His book is called 'The War of the Gaeil [the Irish] with the Gaill [the Foreigners]'. Were those 200 years just one long war between the people of Ireland and the Viking invaders?

The first Viking age

The early Viking raids lasted from 795 to the 850s. At first the Vikings were raiders, but they soon set up permanent bases. Some of their camps gradually became trading towns at Dublin, Waterford, Wexford, Cork and Limerick. From them, the Vikings (or Ostmen as they called themselves) controlled the country around. In many ways they were just like any other little Irish kingdom and were open to attack from the armies of other kings. The Irish found it hard to unite together against them and Irish kings often fought alongside the Ostmen against other Irish kings.

In 846, Máel Sechnaill I became king of Tara. He was one of the greatest kings of the Southern Uí Néill. Soon after he became king Máel Sechnaill defeated the Ostmen in a major battle. But he was not leading a national resistance of Irish against foreign invaders. Máel Sechnaill's territory suffered a lot from Ostmen raids and he was trying to force them to leave his lands in peace, not to drive them out of Ireland.

A The Holy Roman Emperor hears of Máel Sechnaill's victory

1 Why did Méal Sechnaill tell the Emperor about his victory?

2 Prudentius thought this was a victory of Christians over pagan invaders, but it was more complicated than that. In what way?

"848 AD. The Irish attacked the Vikings and were victorious and drove them from their lands, with the help of Our Lord Jesus Christ. Then the king of the Irish sent messengers to the Emperor Charles . . ."

(From Prudentius of Troyes, *Annals of St Bertin*, ninth century)

The second Viking age

Not long after this, the Viking raids died down for many years. Then in 914 large fleets began to arrive again. This time they were not from Scandinavia. The raiders were the sons and grandsons of Vikings who had settled in Scotland, northern England and especially in the Isle of Man and the Hebrides. They put ashore at Waterford and began attacking Munster and Leinster.

B Round Tower at Glendalough, County Wicklow

3 *What does the Irish name tell us about one use of the towers?*

4 *What can you learn from the position of the door?*

5 *What would the higher windows be for?*

6 *How would a building like this reduce the loss of valuables in a raid?*

This time there was a more united effort by the Irish to beat off the raiders. It was led by Niall Glúndubh ('Niall of the Black Knee'). He was king of the Northern Uí Néill and the most powerful province-king in Ireland. He has another claim to fame. Many Irish surnames begin with *Mac* or *O*. The *Mac* means 'son of', the *O* means 'grandson of'. The most famous Irish royal family were the O Neills of Ulster. They and most people with the name O Neill, are descended from this Niall Glúndubh who ruled in the early tenth century.

Niall's home territory was in Tyrone and Derry. What the Vikings were doing down in the south of the country should not have bothered him too much, but like many powerful province-kings Niall wanted to rule all Ireland. He led the resistance to the Vikings as if to show that an attack anywhere in Ireland was his business – that he was 'king of Ireland'. Niall gathered a great army of both Northern and Southern Uí Néill, along with the Ulaid and the Airgialla (see their lands on the map in Unit 7). They marched to Dublin but in the battle fought on 14 September 919 Niall Glúndubh and many other Irish leaders were slain.

For twenty or so years afterwards the Ostmen were very powerful. Then the Irish kings began to get the better of them. The churches recovered from the early attacks and many grew wealthy enough to build large towers which in Irish are called a *cloig-theach* (or bell-house) but today are usually called Round Towers.

Gradually the Ostmen became a normal part of the Irish scene. They had large fleets of ships which Irish kings hired to use against their own enemies. They were especially feared for the heavy iron armour they wore into battle, and their long swords and axes. The Ostmen leaders became Christian and married Irish princesses, while the Irish borrowed Norse names for their children. For example, the common Munster surnames Mac Auliffe and Cotter come from *Mac Amhlaoibh* ('son of Olaf') and *Mac Oitir* ('son of Oitir'). The name Mac Manus or *Mac Maghnuis* comes from one of the Maguire family of Fermanagh who had the Norse name Magnus.

Most important of all, even the name most people now use for our country is a Norse word. The Vikings took the Irish name *Éire* and made it Éire-land or *Ireland*, which in turn became Ireland.

1 *In what ways were the ninth and tenth centuries in Ireland a 'War of the Gaeil with the Gaill'? How can you show that it was sometimes not as simple as that?*

2 *There are over sixty Round Towers in Ireland. Where is the nearest one to you? Find out what you can about it.*

9 Did Brian Boru expel the foreigners?

One of the great heroes of Irish history is Brian Boru. He is remembered today as the king who expelled the Vikings at the Battle of Clontarf in 1014. What do we know about Brian's background and how did he come to be so famous? Did he really expel the Vikings?

The rise of Brian Boru

From the seventh century Munster was ruled by a dynasty called the Eóganacht who kept their power until the middle of the tenth century. Then their rule was challenged by the Dál Cais kings. The Dál Cais had started out as no more than local chiefs in east Clare but in the 960s the family head, Mathgamain, made himself king of north Munster.

Mathgamain's enemies ganged up on him and in 976 captured him and put him to death. They may have thought that was the end of the Dál Cais but they were very much mistaken. Mathgamain's brother, Brian, went after his brother's killers, defeated them all and with great skill got himself made king of all Munster.

Now Brian was a powerful province-king which made him the rival of the other most powerful king, the king of Tara and head of the Uí Néill. He was Máel Sechnaill II who was a direct descendent of Niall of the Nine Hostages, whose family had ruled at Tara even before the time of St Patrick. To him Brian was nothing but an upstart.

In 982 Máel Sechnaill invaded Brian's kingdom and cut down the sacred tree that grew on the spot where the head of the Dál Cais was made king. Máel Sechnaill was trying to show Brian who was boss! But this did little to stop Brian, and the two kings spent many years trying to get the better of each other.

By 997 they held a royal meeting near Clonfert and reached an agreement. Máel Sechnaill would be king over all the northern half of Ireland and Brian would be king of the southern half. But Brian was not happy with this for long. Soon he re-started his war. Finally, in 1002 Máel Sechnaill had had enough. He agreed that Brian should be his overlord and gave him hostages as a sign that he would stay loyal to him.

A Brian's new power, AD 1002

1 *See how many of these Irish kingdoms you can find on the map in Unit 7. Mide means 'the middle' and is now Meath. What is it called on the map?*

2 *Who are the 'foreigners' of Dublin and Waterford? Why are these two towns not marked on the map?*

"A gathering of the men of Mumu, the Connachta, the men of Mide, the Laigin, and of the foreigners of Dublin and Waterford, was made by Brian son of Cennétig, against the Ulaid in order to take their hostages."

(From the *Annals of Inisfallen*)

In 1005 Brian went to Armagh. He gave its clergy twenty ounces of gold and agreed that Armagh would be head of the whole Irish Church. The precious *Book of Armagh* was put on display for the occasion and Brian's secretary wrote into it a record of the visit, calling Brian 'Emperor of the Irish'.

B A page from the *Book of Armagh*

3 Read the sentence in Latin below and see if you can make out any of the writing in the manuscript. (The parts in brackets are left out there to save space.)

4 Calvus Perennis was Brian's secretary. Why do you think he called Brian 'Emperor of the Irish'? Did he deserve the title?

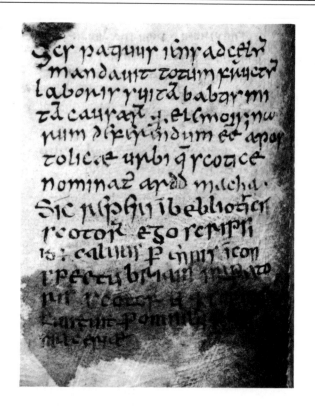

'Ego scripsi, id (est) Calvus P(er)ennis i(n) conspectu Briani Imp(er)atoris Scotor(um)'

which means

'I have written this, that is, Calvus Perennis, in the presence of Brian, Emperor of the Irish'

The Battle of Clontarf

Brian had not been master of all Ireland for long when the king of Leinster and the Ostmen of Dublin rebelled against him. Brian led his armies to invade Leinster and laid Dublin under a siege that lasted for three months until Christmas 1013. Then Brian and his men returned home but the Leinstermen and the Ostmen knew that he would soon be back. So they sent messengers to the Isle of Man and the Scottish Isles and gathered together a vast Viking fleet, ready for Brian's next move.

On Good Friday 1014, they fought Brian's forces at Clontarf in the most famous battle in Irish history. It was a long and bloody event but by evening the Leinstermen and Ostmen had lost. However, as one of them was escaping from the battlefield to his ship, he came across King Brian in his tent. Brian was 73 years old and too weak to fight. The Viking seized his opportunity and assassinated him.

The Vikings who had been called to fight Brian then sailed to their homes. But their Ostmen cousins stayed as rulers of Dublin.

Later a legend grew up that the Battle of Clontarf was fought to see whether the Irish or Vikings would rule Ireland. But Brian probably did not see it in this way. He was fighting the kings of Leinster and Dublin and the Vikings at Clontarf were just paid soldiers called in to help his enemies.

Clontarf was not a power struggle between the Irish and the Ostmen. It was the last stage in Brian's struggle to get all the other province-kings to accept him as king of Ireland. Later members of Brian's family were so proud to be descended from him that they kept the name *Ua Briain* ('grandson of Brian') as a surname. It is now O'Brien and anyone with this name is a direct descendant of Brian Boru.

Brian Boru was an outsider as king of Ireland but overthrew Máel Sechnaill. This was a great shock because Máel Sechnaill's family, the Uí Néill kings of Tara, had been the most powerful kings in Ireland for at least three hundred years. Now Brian showed that any province-king could make himself master over the whole island — if his armies were strong enough.

1 *Explain why Máel Sechnaill thought that Brian Boru was an 'upstart'. Compare their family backgrounds. Do you think Máel Sechnaill was right?*

2 *Give some reasons why the Battle of Clontarf is so important.*

20 Dublin: Capital of Ireland?

For many hundreds of years Dublin has been the biggest city in Ireland and an important centre of government. Where do its origins lie? When and why did it start to become important?

Duibhlinn *and* Áth Cliath

The word Dublin comes from an Irish word *Duibhlinn* which means 'the black pool'. But there is another Irish name for the city which is used more often. That is *Áth Cliath* and means 'the ford of the hurdles'. The ford was on the River Liffey near where the Four Courts are today and it linked the lands of the southern Uí Néill in the north with the Laigin (Leinster) in the south. The hurdles were probably mats made of rods and twigs to help people and animals cross over the muddy ford at low tide. Áth Cliath was a settlement overlooking the ford and several of the main roads of ancient Ireland joined up there.

Duibhlinn takes it name from a black pool on the River Poddle where it joined the Liffey. There was a monastery on the site and there were many churches in the area. One later became St Patrick's Cathedral. The real turning point in Dublin's history came in 841 when the Vikings built a dock at the black pool to shelter their ships. From this base, they could sail up the Liffey to attack the lands and churches of the Southern Uí Néill and the Laigin. It soon became the most important Viking camp in Ireland.

A Map of early Dublin

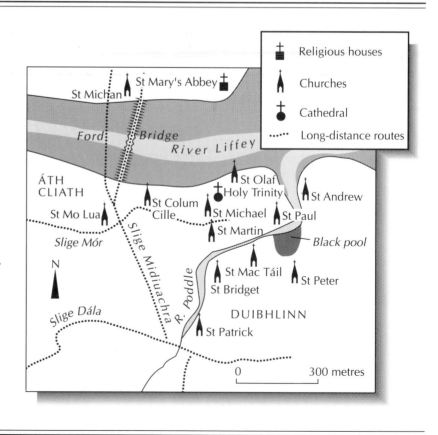

1. What made *Áth Cliath* an important centre of communications?

2. Why did the Vikings first settle at *Duibhlinn* and not *Áth Cliath*?

3. List the churches. Which are called after Irish saints? Are any named after Norse saints? Are any of them still there today?

In the early 1960s, Dublin Corporation decided to build new civic offices at a place along the Liffey called Wood Quay. When the site was being prepared, archaeologists made one of the most exciting discoveries in Ireland's history. Beneath the surface was the original Viking town of Dublin. They found wood that had not yet rotted after 1000 years. They found houses, plots of land, paths, furniture, tools, toys, human skeletons and tons of animal bones, food remains, pottery and clothes. It was enough to piece together the lives of Dublin's first citizens. Eventually the site was destroyed to make way for office blocks.

4 *Explain whether or not you think it was right to build office blocks on Wood Quay.*

Kings and traders

From Duibhlinn the Ostmen conquered all the territory in most of the present County Dublin. The Irish called this little kingdom *Fine Gall* ('the territory of the foreigners') and the name survives in the district of Fingal. The greatest of its kings was Olaf Cuarán. In many ways he was like any Irish king. He married an Irish princess and gave Irish names to some of his children. Like Irish kings he was generous to poets – we still have poems in Irish that were written for Olaf. He was a Christian and retired to spend his last days in the monastery of Iona.

In 989 Olaf's son, Sitric Silkbeard, became king. He started making silver pennies, the first coins ever produced in Ireland. Sitric went on a pilgrimage to Rome in 1028 and when he returned he built what was to become Christ Church Cathedral. He chose an Irishman called Dúnán to be Dublin's first bishop. To show that they were different from the rest of the Irish Church, the Dubliners sent their bishops to England, to be blessed by the archbishop of Canterbury.

Gradually Dublin lost its military power and both Brian Boru and Máel Sechnaill captured the city many times and took away great booty. However Dublin's traders made up for the weakness of its warriors. It became one of the busiest trading ports in western Europe. Irish kings realised this and in 1052 the king of Leinster conquered it and made his son Murchad king, the first native Irish king of Dublin. Murchad is also famous because his descendants were the Mac Murroughs, the best-known of whom was Dermot, who brought the Normans to Ireland.

The city was now so important that when a man became king of Ireland, his next step was to appoint his oldest son to rule Dublin. It was as if he had to serve his apprenticeship as king of Dublin before he too could become king of Ireland. Dublin was becoming the country's capital in everything but name.

Make a list of the reasons why Viking Dublin became the leading town in Ireland.

21 The twelfth-century Church: Irish or European?

In Europe near the end of the eleventh century great changes started to take place in the Church. We call this the Gregorian reform, after Pope Gregory VII who helped start it off. It soon spread to Ireland and brought about many changes in the Church there too. Why were these changes needed? What difference did they make?

Complaints and reforms

When Gregory VII became Pope in 1073, Christianity had been in Ireland for about 650 years. Ireland's isolation from Europe meant that the monks organised their Church quite differently from other countries. Gregory and the other reformers did not like many of the things they were hearing about Ireland, and wanted changes.

They had five main causes of complaint. First, Ireland was not divided up into dioceses and parishes like other countries. Second, abbots had too much power and bishops too little. Third, people outside the Church had too much influence on it. For example, many so-called abbots were not churchmen at all. Their families treated the lands of the monastery as their own property, and handed on the top jobs to their children.

Fourth, churchmen often got married, as we can see from some Irish surnames. The name Taggart or Mac Entaggart is *Mac an tSagairt* ('son of the priest') and Mac Anespie is *Mac an Easpaig* ('son of the bishop'). Fifth, divorce was allowed under Brehon law, and a man could marry his cousin or a relative of his former wife. The reformers did not approve of this. So they got the support of important people in Ireland for a movement to reform the Irish Church. Their leader was the king of Munster, Muirchertach O Brien, a great-grandson of Brian Boru. He was the most powerful province-king and was looked on by many people as king of Ireland.

Muirchertach organised two great gatherings of clergy and lay people to draw up new laws for the Church. These were the Synod of Cashel in 1101 and the Synod of Rath Breasail in 1111. Under these laws, the dioceses that still exist were set up. Monasteries were to be run only by churchmen. Abbots had to be ordained to the priesthood and could not marry.

Muirchertach also gave the Rock of Cashel to the Church. It was to be the Church's headquarters in the southern half of Ireland, as Armagh was in the north. Then, Cormac Mac Carthy, the king of Desmond (or South Munster), built the famous church known as Cormac's Chapel. It was in a style of church building that we call Irish Romanesque. Some things about it were the same as older Irish churches, but it had round arches copied from Roman buildings.

A Cormac's Chapel at Cashel

1 *Nowadays, political leaders do not build churches. Why?*

2 *Why do you think Cormac spent so much money building this church?*

Cormac's Chapel shows that Ireland was coming into close contact with the outside world. In 1123 part of a cross was brought to Ireland which was said to be the cross on which Christ died. The king of Connacht, Turlough O Connor, asked for a small piece and he ordered his craftsmen in Roscommon to make a magnificent bronze cross to hold it. We call this the Cross of Cong. It is the finest work of art produced in Ireland during the time of the Church reforms.

B The Cross of Cong

3 *Do you think Turlough made the cross out of religious devotion or to show what a rich and generous king he was?*

4 *Compare it with the other works of art we have seen in this book. Which is your favourite? Why?*

(The inscription on the cross reads: 'Pray for Turlough O Connor, King of Ireland, for whom this shrine was made')

St Malachy

In 1129, Malachy Ó Morgair, became bishop of Armagh. For many years Armagh had been run by a local family as if it was their own. St Malachy changed that and became the new leader of the reforms.

Ten years later, Malachy went to Rome to ask the Pope to give Ireland its first archbishops. His mission failed but on the way he visited a monastery at Clairvaux in France, run by St Bernard. It was part of a new religious order called the Cistercians. Malachy was so impressed by the monks' simple way of life that he left some of his companions behind to be trained. Later, they returned with some French monks and in 1142 set up the first Cistercian house in Ireland at Mellifont in County Louth.

Eleven more were built over the next twenty years. They brought a new type of religious life into Ireland and a very different kind of monastery from those founded long before by Irish saints. At first, some local people objected, saying 'We are Irish, not French!', but in the end the new Continental monasteries were a great success. They brought Ireland into much closer contact with France and also with the French people who had settled in England after the Norman Conquest in 1066.

Malachy died at Clairvaux in 1148 but he had been to Rome again and at last had got his wish. In 1151 the Pope sent a cardinal to Ireland to hold another Synod. There, the bishops of Armagh, Cashel, Dublin, and Tam became archbishops, with Armagh as head.

The Archbishop of Canterbury did not like Dublin getting its own archbishop, because before that he had some control over the bishop of Dublin – now he was an equal. In 1155, the Archbishop of Canterbury's secretary got a letter from the Pope that gave permission to the king of England, Henry II, to invade Ireland in order to speed up the reforms.

The king came to Ireland in 1171 just after the Norman invasion of Ireland had started. Now, Ireland was added to the many lands under the king of England's control. Henry also held a meeting of the Church at Cashel at which it was agreed that the Irish Church would be run exactly the same way as the Church in England. It was the end of the Irish Church as it had been since the days of Patrick.

1 *Read again the five causes of complaint that the reformers had. Explain which of them you think was the most serious.*

2 *Do you think the changes that took place in the Church in Ireland in the twelfth century were good or bad? Explain your reasons.*

3 *In what way did the reforms help to bring about the Norman invasion of Ireland?*

22 600–1169: What changed?

Brian Boru was one of the great men of Irish history because he came from nowhere to make himself king of Ireland. After him, other province-kings tried to do the same. One hundred and fifty years after Brian's death, the first Normans began to arrive in Ireland, and it became an English colony. Had this anything to do with the changes that Brian brought about?

Ireland and the Church

Remember how isolated Ireland was in AD 600, cut off from the rest of Europe. The Church helped to alter that. In the end, the Irish Church was organised along the same lines as elsewhere, and European religious orders were founding monasteries in Ireland. So it was being brought more and more into contact with Europe instead of being at the edge and out of touch.

Ireland's towns

At the start, Ireland had no towns, but the Vikings changed that. In the end, Ireland had several busy trading towns where Ostmen and Irish people lived side by side, and where Irish kings set up second palaces for themselves. The towns were in close touch with Europe. Dublin was like a sister-city to the English ports of Bristol and Chester. It was a town of great wealth and came to be seen almost as the country's capital.

Ireland's warring kings

In 600 Ireland was a land of many small kingdoms. By 1169 there were only four or five kings who really mattered. The most powerful of them could call himself king of Ireland. For all of this time Ireland was a violent place but people usually only fight if there is something to fight over. In the eleventh and twelfth centuries a province-king went to war for the chance to make himself king of all Ireland.

By the middle of the twelfth century kings kept bigger armies and navies which cost money, so higher taxes were needed. The kings assumed more power and passed laws to force obedience to their rule. They even began to hand out to their friends lands they took from enemies. This happened in other countries, where kings were powerful because of the land they owned or controlled. In Ireland it was new. An Irish king was meant to be the leader of his people, not the owner of their land.

The ambition of King Dermot

When kings looked for ways of increasing their power and wealth they could run into trouble. This happened to Dermot Mac Murrough. In 1166 he had been king of Leinster for over thirty years. In many ways he was an evil and cruel man but he was also a very modern king, with influential friends in Europe, including St Bernard of Clairvaux. St Lorcán (or Laurence) O Toole, the Archbishop of Dublin, was his brother-in-law. He set up new monasteries organised like those in Europe and was strongly in favour of Church reforms.

Dermot also saw himself as king of Dublin because a modern king needed to rule more than farmland; he needed the wealth and the glamour that came from being lord over a famous international trading city. But Dermot had enemies. In 1166, one of them, the Connacht king, Ruairí O Connor, became high-king. To be king of Ireland Ruairí needed Dublin. He gave its citizens 4000 cows which were paid for by the people of Ireland, and the Dubliners agreed to make him their king.

Without the wealth of Dublin or its Ostmen fighters, Dermot was very weak. If he was not such a modern European-minded king he might have accepted Ruairí's power. But not Dermot. He went abroad looking for Norman knights to help him win back his kingdom. In return he offered them land in Ireland. This is how the Normans came to Ireland in 1169. Ever since then all or part of Ireland has been connected to Britain.

A poem about Ireland written by St Donatus in the ninth century:

> *The noblest share of the earth is the far western world*
> *Whose name is written* Scotia *in the ancient books;*
> *Rich in goods, in silver, jewels, cloth and gold,*
> *Benign to the body, in air and mellow soil.*
> *With honey and with milk flow Ireland's lovely plains,*
> *With silk and arms, abundant fruit, with art and men.*
>
> *Worthy are the Irish to dwell in this their land,*
> *A race of men renowned in war, in peace, in faith.*

(Translated by Liam de Paor, *Early Christian Ireland*, 1958)

1 *What have you learned in this book about the following:*

 (a) *Ireland in 'the far western world'*
 (b) *The name 'Scotia'*
 (c) *The 'goods, silver, jewels' and so on found in Ireland long ago?*

2 *Was flowing 'with milk and with honey' an accurate description of Ireland's farming and food-supply? In which ways was it untrue?*

3 *How would you illustrate the statement that 'Ireland's lovely plains' were full of art?*

4 *Was it true that the Irish of St Donatus's time were famous 'in war, in peace, in faith'?*

5 *Make a list of the ten most important things you have learned about Ireland long ago from this book.*